What Magnets Can Do

By Allan Fowler

Consultants

Robert L. Hillerich, Professor Emeritus,
Bowling Green State University, Bowling Green, Ohio;
Consultant, Pinellas County Schools, Florida

Lynne Kepler, Educational Consultant

Fay Robinson, Child Development Specialist

CHILDRENS PRESS®
CHICAGO

Design by Herman Adler Design Group
Photo Research by Feldman & Associates, Inc.

Library of Congress Cataloging-in-Publication Data

Fowler, Allan.
    What magnets can do / by Allan Fowler.
      p. cm. – (Rookie read-about science)
    ISBN 0-516-06034-1
    1. Magnetism—Juvenile literature. 2. Magnets—Juvenile literature.
  [1. Magnetism. 2. Magnets.] I. Title. II. Series.
QC753.7.F69   1995
538–dc20
                                 94-35628
                                     CIP
                                     AC

Why are these nails
sticking to this bar?

They aren't glued on. You'd expect them to fall down. They stick to the bar because the bar is a magnet.

A magnet is a piece of metal that can attract another piece of metal.

The two pieces stick
to each other.

Most magnets are made
of iron or steel. Some
are cobalt or nickel.
And the only metals a
magnet attracts are iron,
steel, cobalt, and nickel.

So you can pick up nails
or paper clips or pins with
a magnet. They are made
of magnetic metals.

Or you can place a magnet
on your refrigerator door.
It will stick there and
hold notes.

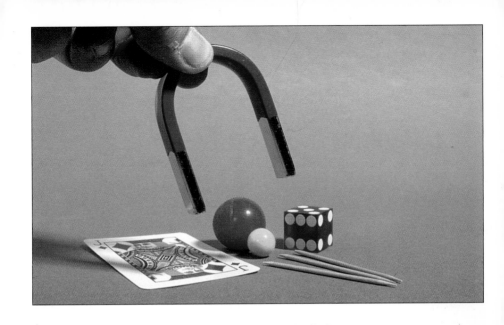

But a magnet won't pick up
a wooden toothpick or a
rubber ball or a plastic die.
It won't stick to a plaster
wall. There are no magnetic
metals in these things.

Magnets can be almost any shape. Some magnets are bars or discs, and some are even shaped like doughnuts.

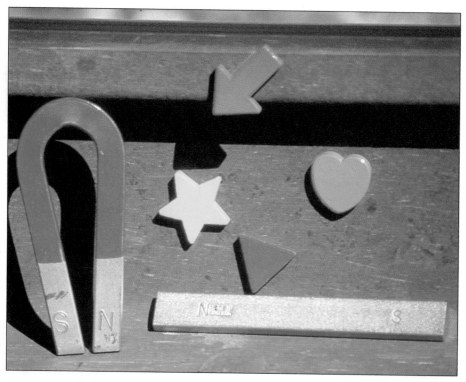

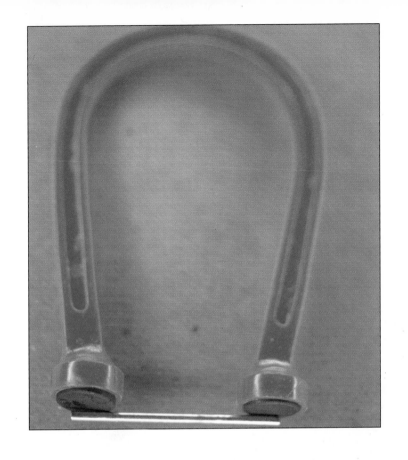

You might have seen a horseshoe magnet, like this one.

But every magnet, no matter what its shape, has a north pole and a south pole.

Let's place two bar magnets with the north pole of one close to the south pole of the other.

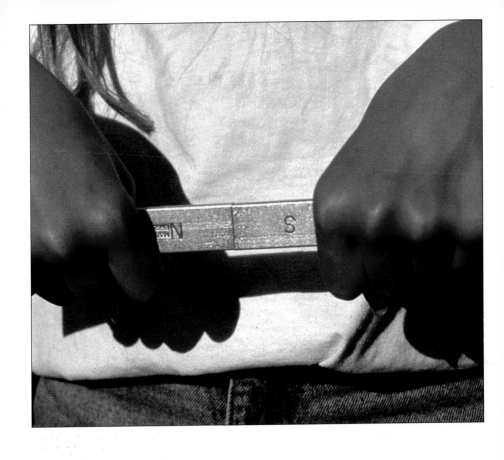

What happens? The
magnets attract each
other and stick together.

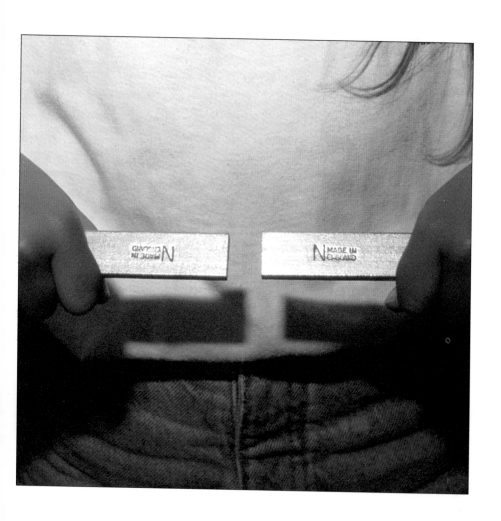

14

If we turn one of them around, the magnets repel each other — they push each other away.

Here is another way to see these magnetic forces.

Hang one magnet from a string. Hold another magnet in your hand. Bring it slowly toward the hanging magnet. What happens?

What happens after you turn one of the magnets around?

18

The needle of a pocket compass is simply a magnet.

A pilot uses a compass to make sure his plane is going in the right direction. So does the captain of a ship.

A compass needle always
points north. Here's why.
The Earth itself is a huge
magnet. And like any
magnet, the Earth has a
north pole and a south pole.

The Earth's north magnetic
pole attracts one end of
the compass needle. Try
turning your pocket compass
around. The needle will
still point north.

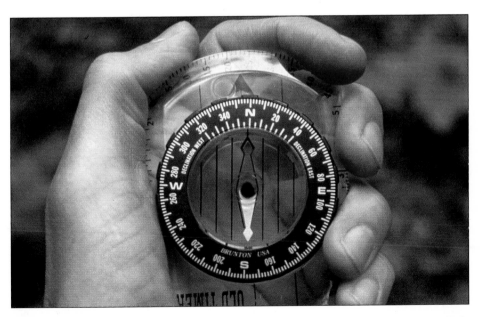

Some magnets can be turned on and off.

When an electric current runs through this wire, the iron bar inside the wire becomes a magnet – an electromagnet.

24

This crane uses an
electromagnet to pick
up heavy pieces of metal.

When the crane operator
wants to drop the metal
on a pile, he just turns
off the electric current.

There are many hidden magnets in your home.

They help your TV and VCR and computer game discs work.

And they are inside your stereo, telephone, vacuum cleaner, refrigerator, washing machine, and other things that run on electricity.

You can make a magnet yourself. Pick up a paper clip with an ordinary magnet. Now see how a second paper clip sticks to the first one.

As long as the first clip is touching the magnet, it becomes a magnet itself.

How long a chain of magnetized paper clips can you make?

29

Words You Know

bar magnet

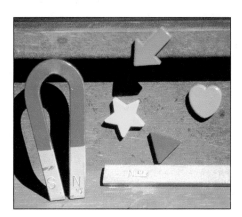

magnets

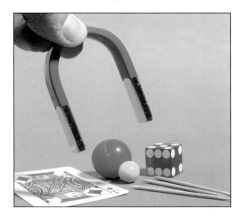

horseshoe magnet

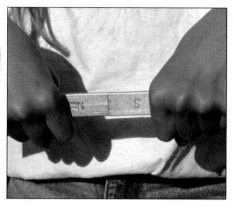

attract

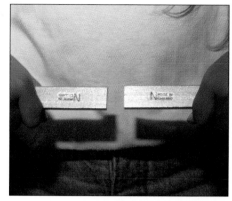

repel

electromagnet

compass

31

Index

About the Author

Allan Fowler is a free-lance writer with a background in advertising. Born in New York, he lives in Chicago now and enjoys traveling.

Photo Credits

PhotoEdit – ©Tony Freeman, 5, 8, 9, 20, 23, 30 (bottom right), 31 (bottom right); ©David Young-Wolff, 6, 27

Photri – 11

Rainbow – ©T.J. Florian, Cover

SuperStock International, Inc. – ©Jerry Atnip, 18

Tony Stone Images – ©Robert E. Daemmrich, 29

Unicorn Stock Photos – ©Jim Shippee, 10, 13, 14, 19, 30 (top right), 31 (top left and top right); ©Rich Baker, 21; ©Joe Sohm, 24, 31 (bottom left)

Valan – ©V. Wilkinson, 3, 17, 30 (left)

COVER: Magnets